HIS CROWN OF JEWELS

VOLUME I

Pearl Edition

GAIL BEECH

HIS CROWN OF JEWELS
VOLUME I PEARL EDITION
by GAIL BEECH

Printed in the United States of America.

ISBN 9781498489942

Unless otherwise indicated, Scripture quotations taken from the King James Version (KJV) – *public domain.*

www.xulonpress.com

DEDICATION

I dedicate the first volume of His Crown of Jewels, the Pearl Edition, to Jesus Christ my Lord and Saviour. This is the first poetry book in a series so the first fruits will go to Him. In each edition, a jewel will be placed into His crown on the cover. Since the pearl represents suffering, it was chosen for this edition as a reminder of the sacrificial love Christ has for us and the sufferings He endured to give us the gift of salvation. I give all credit to Him for filling the pages of this book with poetic insights that can enrich your life.

ACKNOWLEDGMENTS

To my family: I want to thank each of you for your loving support all through the years and for believing in me. Your encouragement means more to me than you'll ever know. I love you all from the depths of my heart. You have each filled my life with love, joy and so much meaning. Thank you for reading and listening to countless hours of poetry. I'm so thankful for each of you.

To Marie Perullo Williams: Thank you for the numerous hours you dedicated to putting scriptures to many of these poems and doing it with a cheerful heart. I appreciate the time you invested listening to poetry and offering your suggestions. Thank you for being there for me through the years, no matter what.

To Sally Bone Fay: It can't go without mention that you edited these poems years ago. Although they've changed since then, thank you for your sacrifice of time. I'll always be grateful for your act of kindness.

To Sarah Fowler, my previous Sunday School teacher who is with the Lord now: Thank you to Ms. Sarah for helping me believe in myself and for the opportunities to share my poetry (reading to our class and giving me some of her space in our church newsletter for poetry).

To All of My Wonderful Friends: Thank you from the depths of my heart for being my friend. I love and appreciate each of you.

~~~THANK YOU EVERYONE FOR YOUR FAITHFUL PRAYERS~~~

TABLE OF CONTENTS

A CREATIVE MIND

Is a creative mind empty or full?
Does it have an outward push or an inward pull?
Must mind be emptied so it can be filled
With creativity that the universe spills?

Or must it be full of knowledge and such
And create within from mind's collection of much?
The talents we have must be found and used
In the place where thoughts and reality are fused.

Journey into the center of your mind
Exploring every crevice that you find
Then layers of truth will be uncovered
And mysteries untold will be discovered.

God created our minds so wonderfully made
And filled them with riches before they were braid.
He put keys to unlock creativity
Within the realm of our own trinity.

The hidden wealth that is stored within
Will spill creative treasures when you let yourself in.
As you challenge yourself right down to the core
Pull strength from within to push open life's door.

Every good gift and every perfect gift is from above,
and cometh down from the Father of lights, with
whom is no variableness, neither shadow of turning.
James 1: 17

A MUSTARD SEED

A little mustard seed
In a little clay pot
Opened up its little eyes
While pushing the ground up top.

Make way for my faith to grow
For it's going to grow up big.
It will shade the mountains of my doubt
For God's "Son" will feed each twig.

The roots searched for holy waters
And rich nutrients of good soil.
When the Holy Spirit was found within
They satisfied their toil.

As the roots of faith were growing
And this tree became mature
The clay pot broke into little pieces
From growing pains and pressure.

Cracked and broken all apart
The clay pot laid upon the ground
Because the seed that had been inside
Is now a tree stretching Heaven bound.

If the pot had not been broken
From the pressure of the roots
The tree of faith could not grow big
And the tree would have no shoots.

Broken pieces of this clay pot
Can no longer be found
Because roots of faith buried them
As they grew in holy ground.

Big faith has no chance to grow
A tree of faith in a little pot
But if you trust the Potter's hand
You'll see it grow more than you thought.

Mountains of doubt seem so small
When sitting in a faith grown tree
Because if you look down to the ground
You won't see your problems though they still be.

If you don't want your clay pot broken
And are satisfied with less
Then you'll have no growing pains
Or tree of faith for God to bless.

31b The kingdom of heaven is like to a grain of mustard
seed, which a man took and sowed in his field: 32 Which
indeed is the least of all seeds: but when it is grown it is
the greatest among herbs, and becometh a tree, so that the
birds of the air come and lodge in the branches thereof.
St. Matthew 13: 31-32

A PRAYERFUL HEART

A prayerful heart with speechless tongue
Is more pleasing to our Lord
Than heartless prayers filled with words
Searching for reward.

A prayerful heart is filled with jewels
And buried treasures to be found
Then as the shovel of praise digs deep in worship
It strikes gold beneath solid prayer ground.

A prayerful heart is one that prays
Without stopping for distraction
Because when Jesus is our Beloved
Intentions to pray take action.

5 And when thou prayest, thou shalt not be as the hypocrites are: for they love to pray standing in the synagogues and in the corners of the streets, that they may be seen of men. Verily I say unto you, They have their reward. 6 But thou, when thou prayest, enter into thy closet, and when thou hast shut thy door, pray to thy Father which is in secret; and thy Father which seeth in secret shall reward thee openly. 7 But when ye pray, use not vain repetitions, as the heathen do: for they think that they shall be heard for their much speaking.
St. Matthew 6: 5-7

ABIDE AND ARISE

Abide…Abide
In me abide
Reveal Thyself
As I am tried.

Arise…Arise
Thyself in me
With holy vision
Let me see.

As You abide
And arise in me
I commit my soul
To follow Thee.

Whosoever transgresseth, and abideth not in the doctrine
of Christ, hath not God. He that abideth in the doctrine
of Christ, he hath both the Father and the Son.
II St. John 1: 9

ALL AT ONE TIME

Lord, please let me die all at one time.
Keep united my body, soul and mind.
I don't want to leave separately
So take me all together is my plea.

We worked together all the days of our life
And finally found Your peace amidst much strife.
It was quite a feat to work in harmony
So please don't take one away from our three.

If you take my body, my mind will feel trapped.
But if you take my mind I'll be real handicapped
Because a body without its mind, will wander around
So they really need each other in order to be sound.

God, I want to be mindful of You till my end
And I don't want any part of me living in pretend.
So in Your goodness please keep us three as one
Till it's time for us to be with You and Your Son.

The Trinity of You is mirrored in me
And the parts that make me whole equal to three.
My body, mind and soul join to make me one
So please don't separate this masterful creation.

*Surely goodness and mercy shall follow me all the days of
my life: and I will dwell in the house of the LORD for ever.
Psalm 23: 6*

ALPHA AND OMEGA LOVE

Dear Alpha and Omega Love,
You were my first Love, now my last.
My heart belongs to you forever
For Your love can't be surpassed.

Your steadfast love steadies me
And makes me strong when I am weak.
I love to put salvation's joy
Upon my smiling cheeks.

I'll stand upon the Cornerstone
Of Alpha and Omega's Rock
As grace and mercy cement my faith
To make me a building block.

I am Alpha and Omega, the beginning
and the end, the first and the last.
Revelation 22: 13

AMERICA ON 9-11-01

Freedom Bells awakened us to go about our day
Until we heard the tragic news that filled us with dismay.
Tragedy unmerited while innocent were slain
Made us gaze into the skies to see the flame of shock's remain.

As four planes and their passengers crashed into our lives
The freedoms that our nation knew fell victim to the skies.
Disbelief and horror found hate burning on our sod
How could terrorists believe that this could please their god?

When the terrorists took a bite from our Big Apple they could see
That all our seeds of freedom are in a core of loyalty.
We stood united as our tears fell for New York's fallen towers
As thick clouds of sorrow tried to weaken our country's powers.

While we watched through tearful eyes our vision became clear
That we must fight the war on terror so we can live without fear.
The scorching of our future dreams made reality surreal.
How could towers tumble with a heart that's made of steel?

As the world watched in silence, did hope for peace grow dim
While loved ones laid in rubble till the cement swallowed them?
When the twins tore apart and crumbled to ground zero
Our freedom bell rang louder for each succumbed hero.

We honor those on Flight 93 because they sacrificed their lives
And fought the terrorists on the plane so others could survive.
Though the Pentagon was damaged and lives were lost there too
Our Eagle proudly soars in skies of red, white and blue.

With our media ablazed all nations could behold
Lighting of the justice torch that our President will hold.
Lives that left an imprint and the heroes that arose
Have been our blessings of the blaze whose flame forever glows.

While smoldering the minds of our country in dire need
Frozen within smoke and fire will be our memories indeed.
We fan the flames of tragedy as our hearts burn with prayer
And ask the God of mercy to let us breathe war-free air.

*If my people, which are called by my name, shall
humble themselves, and pray, and seek my face, and
turn from their wicked ways; then will I hear from
heaven, and will forgive their sin, and will heal their land.
II Chronicles 7: 14*

ANGEL BABIES AND HEAVEN'S FLOWERS

In the nighttime shadows when the sun takes rest
You'll find angel babies playing in grassy nests.
They love to play on earth at night since they light up and glow
So angels come with them to watch their playful light show.

Heaven has no darkness, so they don't know they brightly shine
Until they come to earth to play where they also learn about mankind.
Grown angels teach them as they play about the things of this world
And their very favorite lessons are about God's boys and girls.

When morning arrives and the sunlight shines on them
All the angels spread their wings and fly back up to Him.
And where each adorable little angel baby played
Beautiful flowers bloom in the sun's glistening cascade.

Painted in colorful petals, each blooming flower smiles
As they gaze the heavenly skies across the clouded blue miles.
Every garden loves it when angel babies come their way to play
Because the fragrance of Heaven gets on those flowers to stay.

Each and every flower whose lovely petals dry and fall
Will bloom someday in Heaven because angel babies collect them all.
Every blossom has excitement knowing their day will come
To be a beautiful flower in the "Son-light" of God's garden kingdom.

If you love to plant flowers in the potting soil of earth
Don't worry when their petals fall because they'll get rebirthed.
When angel babies come back daily on our behalf to pray
They'll take our fallen flowers with them beyond the stars each day.

When flowers get to Heaven they're given new blossom gowns
With unmatched beauty to decorate Heaven's holy grounds.
Then once dressed, each flower begins to happily sing
Because they're given voices so they can praise Christ our King.

Then angel babies gather the worshipping flowers in each wing
And present them to the Lord so He can hear the petaled chorus sing.

He delights in flower praises and laughs with great joy
Because He knows they're in Heaven forevermore to enjoy.

When flowers see their reflection in the Lord's shiny crown
Tears of happiness that look like dew fall on their heavenly gown.
After the flowers worship the Lord they are taken outside
And shown around Heaven with angel babies at their side.

Uncountable rows of flowers lined up cheek to cheek
Harmonize in fragrant worship perfuming each word they speak.
Their praises are so beautiful that all the angels sing along
As His throne room is sweetened with each scented flower song.

Since Heaven's flowers are given a glorious voice so they can sing
They are no longer considered to be a powerless, fragile weakling.
Their roots grow strong and deep because when they give God praise
It keeps them grounded while the roof gets raised.

Angel babies fill Heaven's fields with colorful blooming flowers
That make worship sweeter when their scented voice joins ours.
Heaven resonates with Love that saturates the atmosphere
And purifies all hearts to draw lovers of His Love near.

Someday your flowers will greet you when it's your turn to arrive
Into the fullness of Heaven where Love makes everything thrive.
They'll proudly show you their petals of glory that magnify The King
Then surprise you with a bouquet of voices as they begin to sing.

You'll meet the angel babies that tended your flowers for you
Then right before your eyes they'll show you how much they grew.
Before you can blink, they'll transform into mighty Angels of Light
Then a new crop of angel babies will want to play on earth all night!

Consider the lilies how they grow: they toil not,
they spin not; and yet I say unto you, that Solomon
in all his glory was not arrayed like one of these.
St. Luke 12: 27

ANOTHER MOUNTAIN

Another mountain I'm going to conquer
Because I know I'll climb those rocky slopes.
I'm determined to reach the very top
To see how faith can climb my hopes.

Rocky are my hopes at times
While looking to the mountaintop
But step by step my faith continues
Climbing higher without stop.

When faith reached its mountain peak
And embraced my hopes with open arms
I opened up my eyes then saw
Another mountain to my alarm.

God made that mountain, so again I'll climb
And higher will my faith now grow
Because when I finally reach that sky bound top
I'll have greater substance than I now know.

The Lord is my portion, saith my soul; therefore will I hope in him.
Lamentations 3: 24

ASLEEP BY A MANGER

Asleep by a manger
Laying in hay
Mary is waiting
For Christmas Day.

Sitting by a manger
Mary will soon find
Her baby is coming
To save mankind.

Resting by a manger
Bundled in joy
Mother of Jesus
Will birth God's boy.

Worship by a manger
Virgin of grace
Bearing God's child
For the human race.

Waiting by a manger
Our coming Saviour
Prepares the time
For Mary's labor.

Ready by a manger
Our Saviour to be
Journeys into time
From eternity.

Praying by a manger
Waiting to be born
Star of Bethlehem
Shine for His adorn.

Asleep by a manger
Awakened by God
Baby Jesus is coming
On warm hay sod.

Awake in a manger
Born to die
For the sins of man
Baby don't cry.

For unto you is born this day in the city of
David a Saviour, which is Christ the Lord.
St. Luke 2: 11

BEING IN OUR ATTITUDES

Blessed are they that donated their goods
Giving to others all that they could
Visiting the sick and delivering meals
Praying to God for others to heal.

Blessed are they that volunteered their time
To work without pay to honor our Divine
Listening to others to help calm fears
And always willing to lend their ears.

Blessed are they who can cry for others
Tears of compassion for one another
Those who are willing to lend a helping hand
To the wounded and hurting who alone can't stand.

Blessed are they who are humble to all
As they reach out to others to help break their fall.
The warmth of their smiles brings comfort within
To the downtrod, outcast and lonely in sin.

Blessed are they who speak with kind words
And show God's love so that actions can be heard
Those that feed the hungry and tend man's needs first
Then share the gospel after quenching their thirst.

Blessed are they who can forgive all wrongs
Releasing pains to Christ, where they belong
Because arms free of burden can reach out in deed
To help carry others in their time of need.

Blessed are they who are criticized for Christ's sake
And bear every insult and suffering they take.
Rewards wait in Heaven so rejoice and be glad
For every tribulation on earth that you've had.

Blessed are they whose faith does not falter
For those are the ones you'll find at God's altar.
They pray through times that are both bad and good
Giving thanks for all things, though all aren't understood.

Being in our attitudes means being in His
And not judging others by the way that they live.
Our lives should reflect just what Christ would do…
Love sinners and lead them to Calvary through you.

St. Matthew 5: 1-12

BIBLE BONES

The old bones of the Bible
Have good meat on them.
From Genesis to Malachi
Come eat and feast with Him.

These bones have not been petrified
Though old all thirty nine.
They have fresh meat to be eaten
With New Testament Bread and Wine.

So fill your belly with sweet meat
As Bible Bones are indulged
Then you'll find faith's bony soul
Is strong with marrow bulged.

Faith's muscles when exercised
Support convictions to stand tall
And fortified Bible bones
Protect us from sin's brittle fall.

Once you've passed through Heaven's gate
You'll be honored with a feast.
You'll meet The Bread, Wine and Bible Bones
While you dine with The High Priest.

*13 For every one that useth milk is unskilful in the word of
righteousness: for he is a babe. 14 But strong meat belongeth
to them that are of full age, even those who by reason of use
have their senses exercised to discern both good and evil.
Hebrews 5: 13-14*

*24 And when he had given thanks, he brake it, and said, Take, eat:
this is my body, which is broken for you: this do in remembrance
of me. 25 After the same manner also he took the cup, when
he had supped, saying, This cup is the new testament in my
blood: this do ye, as oft as ye drink it, in remembrance of me.
I Corinthians 11: 24-25*

BY EXAMPLE

When ridiculed and laughed at
Because you're trying to live right
Prayerfully hold your chin up
And always stand upright.

By example the way you live
Is sowing seeds all the while
Into the hearts of those you know
So grow them with a smile.

Those who want to tear you down
Just want to see you fall
But if you love the Lord
Don't let them bother you at all.

When harvest time arrives
Everything you said or did
Will bear fruit for the Lord
So don't let your life be hid.

He that followeth after righteousness and
mercy findeth life, righteousness, and honour.
Proverbs 21: 21

CHARITABLE LOVE

Charity is the union of love and deeds
Joining hearts and souls to follow Christ's lead.
It's the beautiful wings that makes love fly
And the gentle compassion that draws Him nigh.

Charity is love and good will to men.
It's the powerful force that tames selfish sin.
Charity suffers alongside a friend
With loving devotion without end.

Love is not puffy yet certainly swells
Spilling joy from each heart where Jesus indwells.
Kind words and deeds can surely defeat sin
When love put into action speaks from within.

It is tender words with a righteous voice
And integrity used when making a choice.
Faith, hope and deeds without love will not stand
For it's charity that makes loving so grand.

Desires for material things will fade
As you begin to see where your treasures are laid.
Reach for your neighbors without greedy hands
And offer to help them whenever you can.

Be not easily provoked for love's sake
So those around you will know without mistake
That your strength is to the glory of Christ
Who poured charity into love's sacrifice.

Bear, hope, believe and endure in all things
Knowing that our Father brings you blessings.
Rejoicing where truth and justice prevail
Is the charity of love that cannot fail.

Mankind's Saviour who went to Calvary
Opened His arms to fill love with charity.
Though we only know of Him now in part
Someday, face to face, we'll see Love's perfect heart.

The spectrum of love reflected through Him
Shows His true colors and never grows dim.
Honor God's love and behave properly
And your true colors will shine eternally.

A glimpse of His kingdom through love in action
Fills hearts with desire for divine interaction.
Remain true to faith, hope and charity
Knowing that charity is the greatest of the three.

I Corinthians 13: 1-13

CHIMED VOICE

Chimed voice, church bell sing
Proclaim our Saviour's song.
Unprejudiced to every ear
Ring salvation near.

Chimed voice of atmosphere
With messages in song
In stillness victory waits its toll
Church bell ring and wake lost souls.

Message for repentant ears
Awake from sinner's sleep
Heavy laden weeper sings
When salvation rings.

Midnight song, stroke of twelve
Chime, confession, chime.
Tolls of darkness dissipate
Salvation is at stake.

Chimed voice, now hour of truth
Redemptive stroke of One
Evil-doer sleepers wake
Eternal judgment now to take.

Chimed voice, church bell ring
Victorious melody
Universal sound waves
Filled with chimes of praise.

Proclamation of the Heavens
Eternal bell forever chime
Resonate with songs of love
To celebrate our Beloved.

*11 And that, knowing the time, that now it is high time to awake
out of sleep: for now is our salvation nearer than when we believed.
12 The night is far spent, the day is at hand: let us therefore cast
off the works of darkness, and let us put on the armour of light.
Romans 13: 11-12*

CHRISTMAS SHOPPERS

T'was the day before Christmas
And all through the town
Everyone was out shopping
For good deals to be found.

Red stickers were reduced
More than just the day before
So businesses could rid themselves
Of excesses in their store.

Shoppers were enticed
With coupons to spend
All the while being tempted
In a frenzy without end.

Nativity scenes and candy
Toys and many clothes
Are drastically reduced
Nearer to day's close.

People were dashing and prancing
Frantically through the aisles
Buying Merry Christmas gifts
Wearing frowns all the while.

Christmas carols were playing
To bring good cheer to all
As register bells were ringing
Till the closing of the mall.

Dollar bills kept on piling
Into stuffed register drawers
Until the clock's final toll
T'was time to lock the stores.

Not a moment too late
Everyone dashed from the mall
Christmas Eve is almost over
Don't forget the wrapping paper, y'all.

On the sleigh of the night
Guided by a golden shiny nose
The bright full moon is glowing
As excitement at home grows.

There's no time for church
Or candle light prayers
Because the wrapping of gifts
Is the first of their cares.

They were cooking till wee hours
And wrapping gifts…more, more, more
Till on the morn of their awaited Christmas
All you could hear was snore-grunt-snore.

All nestled asleep inside of dreams
With each shopper passed out in bed
This Christmas Day is almost over
Before they raised their sleepy head.

With overcooked turkeys
And smoldering mad dads
Oh no!!! The gifts from Santa
Are still in shopping bags.

Christmas joy was gone
In the teary eyed little kids
And everyone was red hot
While blowing steam off their lids.

We gave thanks for burned food
And casseroles of black
Then said, "The heck with the hoopla,
Let's bring Jesus back!"

The holiday traditions
Had ruined this celebrated day
So from now on each Christmas
We'll worship Christ and pray.

By example we'll show others
All the lessons learned this season
And that Christmas should be merry
Because Jesus 'tis the reason!

*Behold, a virgin shall be with child, and shall
bring forth a son, and they shall call his name
Emmanuel, which being interpreted is, God with us.
St. Matthew 1: 23*

CHURCH PEOPLE

Beautiful to look at
When sitting on the pews
Are all of God's church people
Just waiting to be used.

They've been sitting on the same pew
Every Sunday for years
Listening to good preaching
Shouting amen and cheers.

In one ear and out the other
After a sermon with heart prick
The church people start heading home
But the preacher's words don't stick.

What's for lunch? Is it naptime?
Yes, the busies of church day
Seem to occupy the saints
Instead of seeking time to pray.

Kicked back in the recliner
They have the remote in one hand
And in the other will be found
Liquid happiness that's canned.

The day was good and peaceful
With lots of food and drink
But when it's time for night service
There's too much to do, they think.

Once church clothes are taken off
They won't be put back on the back
Instead, they'll hang till next Sunday
On the "nice clothes only" rack.

Once a week is just enough
For most church go-ers when they go
But do church people realize
That they will reap what they sow?

So if they haven't given tithes
Served the Lord or given praise
Then church people should look inside
And change their "churchy" ways.

And moreover, because the preacher was wise, he
still taught the people knowledge; yea, he gave good
heed, and sought out, and set in order many proverbs.
Ecclesiastes 12: 9

CLAPPING HANDS

Too tired to lift my hands in praise
So I laid them on my lap
But then the Holy Spirit said
"Arise, oh hands and clap!"

I asked for strength as they were raised
While I began to sing
Then my hands joined into worship
With their joyful clapping.

The joy of the Lord is my strength
Hallelujah...He's my King!!!
My hands now love to join together
For their worship offering.

Lift up your hands in the sanctuary, and bless the Lord.
Psalms 134: 2

COMMUNION

The taste of a cracker
Never tasted so grand
As when it represents
Your body in my hand.

When I place it in my mouth
I give all thanks to You
For every healing I receive
As I begin to chew.

I think of all the stripes
And ridicule You took
As it is recorded
In The Living Book.

You were beaten for mankind
To heal and set us free
Yet with all the sufferings You endured
You still went to Calvary's tree.

Now in Your remembrance
I drink from the cup
That represents Your shed blood
As I take my Lord's sup.

Without nails in Your sacrifice
My sins would not be covered
So thank You Jesus, for salvation
And that my soul has been recovered.

For as often as ye eat this bread, and drink this
cup, ye do shew the Lord's death till he come.
I Corinthians 11: 26

CONVERSATION'S GOOSE

Hot lips of rampant temper
And tongue's meltdown of abuse
Have allowed flames of anger
To cook conversation's goose.

Before each word gets crispy
From the searing of tongue's grill
Walk away from arguments
And keep your own tongue cool and still.

Then anger's flame will have no fuel
And no one to crank up the heat
Because the appetite to talk is gone
Since burnt words have no meat.

An ungodly man diggeth up evil: and
in his lips there is as a burning fire.
Proverbs 16: 27

CRYSTAL RIVER

There is a Crystal River that sparkles from above
Freshly filled with Living Waters from currents of God's love.

Like brilliant polished diamonds flowing through Heaven's doors
Each drop is headed into lives that want to clean their shores.

Those who ask for our Saviour to dredge their hearts of sin
Receive the Crystal Waters with a gentle rushing in.

Drench yourself in this pureness, the light of dawn's new day
Then bask in glory full of glitter where crystals form in clay.

Drink from joy that refreshes where thirst is quenched indeed
By irrigating souls of others through helping those in need.

When tides of praise start to rise prepare to celebrate
As ripples of His Love start overflowing through your gate.

But when ebb tide approaches submerge yourself in prayer
Then by faith the weak will rise through swells of tender care.

Sunlight painted waters, reflecting clouded sky and slope
Are mirrors of eternal bliss with pristine rays of hope.

The iridescent riverbed filled with gold and jewels
Will lead us to His shining throne where grace and mercy rules.

When you climb the river banks you'll stand at Heaven's door
Embraced by One called Crystal River that washed upon your shore.

And he shewed me a pure river of water of life, clear as
crystal, proceeding out of the throne of God and of the Lamb.
Revelation 22: 1

DEPRESSION'S COCOON

Silence in the walls of darkness
Is sheltering mind's cocoon, depressed.
Accumulating gradually
Was cocoon of sadness spun by me?

Out of fear I locked out joy
Afraid its happiness I'd destroy.
Mental anguish intruding me
Visits my life too regularly.

While spinning threads of hopelessness
My somber chambers can't find rest.
Days of darkness light up my gloom
By shining sadness into mind's room.

My life's been given to the Lord
But the devil wants my mind to hoard.
A shelter built to hide what's left
Is my protection from sorrow's theft.

All my friendships have been smothered
So now I stay away from others.
I find my withered self alone
Picking weeds that loneliness has grown.

As walls thicken to withstand pain
I start to notice that something's changed.
My silken case no longer fits
And darkness is fading bit by bit.

I know the time is opportune
So I'm wiggling out of my cocoon.
The silent moans of every prayer
Have been absorbed by His gracious care.

Transformation within the soul
Brings metamorphosis to my whole.
Now I'm free as a butterfly
And with wings of peace my mind can fly.

These things I have spoken unto you, that in me ye might
have peace. In the world ye shall have tribulation:
but be of good cheer; I have overcome the world.
St. John 16: 33

DESTINY SHOES

When daily walking with the Lord
Wear destiny shoes upon your feet.
If you don't walk ahead or behind
Then you'll arrive without defeat.

Destiny shoes on obedient feet
Give confidence to walk upright
So dare not take your shoes off
Because they were made for His delight.

If you don't know where to go
And your pathway is hard to see
You must step out and walk in faith
Then He can lead you on your journey.

If you end up doing nothing
Because you don't know what to do
Then He can't guide the steps you take
So start walking and He'll give you a clue.

Walk in His Light while in the land of the living
And serve Him with gladness then you will see
That though the pathway is long and narrow
You're never alone on life's journey.

Don't let your destiny shoes be destined
To show no wear on their treads
Because as you get older you'll have regrets
If you wore other shoes instead.

Someday when you stand before Jesus
He'll check your destiny shoes for wear and tear.
If He sees that the tread was wisely used
He'll crown your feet with an everlasting pair.

*8 For thou hast delivered my soul from death,
mine eyes from tears, and my feet from falling. 9 I
will walk before the LORD in the land of the living.
Psalm 116: 8-9*

DEVOUT

Hollow hearts
Hollow words
Unfulfilled
Unheard.

God's passion
God's voice
Freedom
Rejoice.

Love in
Love out
Lovingly
Devout.

*2 A devout man, and one that feared God with all his house, which
gave much alms to the people, and prayed to God alway. 3 He saw
in a vision evidently about the ninth hour of the day an angel of God
coming in to him, and saying unto him, Cornelius. 4 And when he looked
on him, he was afraid, and said, What is it, Lord? And he said unto him,
Thy prayers and thine alms are come up for a memorial before God.
Acts 10: 2-4*

DIVINE MATH

Salvation is the most important
Math problem we each must solve.
The answer is found by looking within
So let's learn divine math and get rid of our sin.

When salvation is added unto someone
Their sin is subtracted from their whole.
Their remainder is counted as part of The One
Who created the equation of salvation.

The Father, Son and Holy Spirit are not added unto us
But are multiplied for our deliverance
So by divine math, you'll soon see
That three times one equals Christ in me.

The only fraction that we must learn
Is how to reduce our selfish parts.
The fragments of self are reduced by God's Son
Until self is gone and there remains just One.

Living for Christ requires some division
But the only rule that we must learn
Is to divide ourselves away from sin
Or else we'll be divided from within.

Do the math of our Divine
So that you don't miscalculate
The sum of sin plus God's wrath
Or you'll find that you flunked earth math.

Lord, tutor us in Your math salvation
Then count our steps as righteousness.
Help us understand Your divine numbers
And to live mathematically unencumbered.

Addition
But seek ye first the kingdom of God, and his righteousness;
and all these things shall be added unto you.
St. Matthew 6: 33

Subtraction
Behold the Lamb of God, which
taketh away the sin of the world.
St. John 1: 29b

Multiplication
Mercy unto you, and peace, and love, be multiplied.
Jude 2

Division
But he, knowing their thoughts, said unto them,
Every kingdom divided against itself is brought to
desolation; and a house divided against a house falleth.
St. Luke 11: 17

DROPS

Death

Resurrection

Our

Personal

Saviour

DEATH

*8 But God commendeth his love toward us,
in that, while we were yet sinners, Christ died for
us. 9 Much more then, being now justified by his
blood, we shall be saved from wrath through him.
Romans 5: 8-9*

RESURRECTION

*3 Concerning his Son Jesus Christ our Lord, which was
made of the seed of David according to the flesh; 4 And
declared to be the Son of God with power, according to
the spirit of holiness, by the resurrection from the dead
Romans 1: 3-4*

OUR SAVIOUR

*4 But after that the kindness and love of God our Saviour toward
man appeared, 5 Not by works of righteousness which we have
done, but according to his mercy he saved us, by the washing
of regeneration, and renewing of the Holy Ghost; 6 Which
he shed on us abundantly through Jesus Christ our Saviour
Titus 3: 4-6*

PERSONAL SAVIOUR

*But if we walk in the light, as he is in the light, we
have fellowship one with another, and the blood
of Jesus Christ his Son cleanseth us from all sin.
1 St. John 1: 7*

SAVIOUR

*And we have seen and do testify that the Father
sent the Son to be the Saviour of the world.
1 St. John 4: 14*

ECHOES OF WORSHIP

Hiding in the secret places
Worship echoes in my heart
You are worthy Lord my God
The great I AM thou art.

Echoes of your name sweet Jesus
In me do abide
Because You alone are worthy of
The praises of Your church and bride.

You are worthy! You are worthy!
Jewel of Salvation shine
Take the heart gems of my worship
And count it precious treasure find.

A good man out of the good treasure of his heart bringeth
forth that which is good; and an evil man out of the evil
treasure of his heart bringeth forth that which is evil:
for of the abundance of the heart his mouth speaketh.
St. Luke 6: 45

ENDANGERED SPECIES

God's little lambs are an endangered species
So angels are sent to protect their "fleece-ies".
Wolves in sheep's clothing are searching for strays
So don't wander from the flock or you may become prey.

Christ gives us warnings which we must heed
So be careful and follow our Shepherd's lead.
Be wise as serpents the Lord says to be
And harmless as doves accordingly.

Beware in all things and be strong in His flock.
Graze on God's Word and become "alive-stock".
His Word is living and will live in each lamb
That stays in the sheepfold of the great I AM.

Behold, I send you forth as sheep in the midst of wolves:
be ye therefore wise as serpents, and harmless as doves.
St. Matthew 10: 16

EVERY THOUGHT

If every thought that's created
Inside our hidden mind
Was made known to others
What good would mankind find?

Would they come to us for counsel
Because Godly wisdom they could see?
Or would we hide in shame's disgrace
And owe others an apology?

Would they know that we're sincere
And that our motives are pure?
Or would they see a double standard
With our words, thoughts and character?

Our every thought is made known
And is not hidden from the Lord
So protect your thoughts and mind
And guard them with your prayer sword.

*23 Search me, O God, and know my heart: try me,
and know my thoughts: 24 And see if there be any
wicked way in me, and lead me in the way everlasting.
Psalm 139: 23-24*

FATHER OF CREATION

Father of Creation
Create Your heart in me
So I can love others
Unconditionally.

Father of Creation
Create Your mind in mine
Help me to understand
Your purposes divine.

Father of Creation
Create within my soul
Courage to live for You
And faith to give You control.

Father of Creation
Please help me to create
Good pleasure for my King
Through worship that is great.

Create in me a clean heart, O God;
and renew a right spirit within me.
Psalms 51: 10

FEAST WITH GOD

God prepared a feast today
So come and fill your plate.
There's love, joy and many fruits
When you celebrate.

Help yourself to all you want
Come feast with God each day.
Healthy souls grow up in Christ
So feed them full without delay.

Love the truth and peace of God
Pray and give thanksgiving
And if you live your life for others
You'll feast in cheerful living.

*shall be to the house of Judah joy and gladness, and
cheerful feasts; therefore love the truth and peace.
Zechariah 8: 19b*

FIRST FRUITS OF EACH DAY

Womb of morning birth in me
A day to worship and glorify Thee.
Lubricate Your joyous dew
And soften each heart it drips into.

Let the first fruits of each day I wake
Fill Your belly with great praise intake.
Awaken my voice with praise and song
Put prayer on my breath and let it be strong.

Sweeten with kindness each word that I say
As they pass from my mouth into Your heart today.
Keep me mindful of You all day long
Because with You is where my thoughts belong.

Each season of life will bear its fruit
But let them all be in worship pursuit
Because You alone will taste the firsts
With the sweetest meat and juiciest squirts.

Of his own will begat he us with the word of truth,
that we should be a kind of firstfruits of his creatures.
James 1: 18

FISH TALE

What a bony little fish
That lays upon my platter.
Since you have no meat to eat
You've been buried in egg batter.

Instead of being fried
You belong back in the sea
But then all your friends would know
What a skimpy meal you made for me.

You're too small to defend yourself
So t'was the fisherman to blame
But if you would have been thrown back
I'd have no "fish tale" for tongue's flame.

I really don't have bragging rights
Although my fishing story seems to grow
So if we both keep our little secret
We'll be the only two that have to know.

I wish you would have swam away
And never swallowed my hook
So you could have grown into a chance
To be a beauty in my scrapbook.

Once you're cast into my belly
Then the story of my flaming tongue
Will spread like wildfire to my friends
Of the "big un" that I strung.

But now I know that I'm hooked
On each fish tale that I fry
Because the flaming stories of my tongue
Are all battered with thick lies.

My lies were told so that like my fish
I'd be bigger than I really am
Yet five loaves and some little fish
Once fed the multitudes by God's Lamb.

Little fish can bring big miracles
Just like the one in my belly
For this little fella sank his hook
Into my heart of sin, though smelly.

That little fish had big tugs
As the Lord worked on my heart.
I fought real hard till too tired
Then quit before I was pulled apart.

Lord forgive me and let my bony fish
Taste better in the oil of truth
And thank You that my little fish
Was wise in his youth.

I'm glad I wasn't thrown back in
To the sea of sinful folly
Because now I'll be a fisherman
And fish for men with my heart's jolly.

The joy of the Lord gives me strength
As I cast the lines of God
Then when the Holy Spirit hooks someone
I'll reel them onto holy sod.

No soul of man will be cast back
No matter what the size
For every soul is important
When seen through God's eyes.

I've finally learned that fish taste better
Without the batter of deceit
And that we should not fish for attention
With bitter words that seem sweet.

The tale I learned from my little fish
Is not to fish with tongue bait
And not to lie or stretch the truth
Because honesty tastes great.

Though I ate my little fish
It's the biggest one I've caught by far
For the taste of truth in my belly
Makes it my trophy memoir.

The words of a talebearer are as wounds, and
they go down into the innermost parts of the belly.
Proverbs 26: 22

FISHIN' AT THE MISSION

Homeless and hungry in line at the mission
While waitin' for a plate of somebody's fishin'
I distanced myself then started filling my belly
Then someone offered me warm biscuits and jelly.

Looking away as I accepted the food
Silence spoke for me though I know this was rude.
I don't know why but she asked to sit with me
A nod of my head was answer to her plea.

My head hung in shame while eating the free meal
Thinking of the mess I'm in seemed surreal.
Now why would this lady want to sit and chat?
I've nothing to offer, she can surely see that.

Then she pulled up a seat while smiling at me
And set down a glass of Southern sweet tea.
In quiet conversation she asked my name
But being so nervous I did not the same.

She claimed to be here to serve a risen Lord
But I didn't know Him so it was ignored.
She kept on serving me like I was a king
And had willingness to bring me anything.

It was her gentleness that lifted me up
As smiles began to surface while we both supped.
She nibbled on biscuits and sipped on sweet tea
Then told me Jesus was watching over me.

A burden was lifted for I now have a friend
At least that's one problem that's starting to mend.
When she looked in my eyes my heart was revealed
Because something about her made me let down my shield.

Before she left the table she prayed for me
Then led me in a sinner's prayer that set me free.
I asked Jesus to forgive me of each sin
And got so excited I said "C'mon in!"

With a promise to come back to visit soon
This lady left so I could kneel in my room.
I don't know her name so "Angel" it will be
And what a good fisherman, I guarantee!

She left work early on the very next day
And put a sign on her door "Gone Fishin' Today"
So if you happen to need her just come and see
She's "fishin' at the mission" for Calvary.

And Jesus said unto them, Come ye after me,
and I will make you to become fishers of men.
St. Mark 1: 17

FISHING IN MIND'S SEA

Fresh ideas are like fresh fish
That are swimming in mind's sea.
You'll catch one if you go fishing
With the hook of creativity.

A real good catch may not be easy
But just tug on hunches and reel them in
Then when you take it off your hook
Someday you'll find yourself a win.

A fine catch one day you'll have
Though ideas may struggle or pull back
But the "big un's" in there, so don't give up
Because you can't fish with faith that's lack.

Feed your mind when it gets hungry
So your ideas can grow and multiply.
Read books and expand your knowledge
Then practice fishing with mind's trained eye.

If your dreams and visions are like-minded
Your imagination will help them grow.
Then one fine day, you'll catch the "big un"
And it ain't gonna be no minnow!!!

Commit thy works unto the LORD,
and thy thoughts shall be established.
Proverbs 16: 3

FOR BLESSED ARE THEY

When the Spirit of God is on the move
Release yourself to go with the flow.
Submit every part unto His desires
For blessed are they who follow.

When the call of God is on your life
Respond to your heart when you feel Him stir.
Resist the struggle that would deny the Lord
For blessed are they that answer.

When the walking stones upon your path
Are covered in dirt and can't be seen
Stop so you don't walk the wrong way
For blessed are they whose steps are kept clean.

When you have a question that needs an answer
And you don't know what to do
Prayerfully wait upon the Lord
For blessed are they who are patient and true.

When you want to live a righteous life
But the ways of the world weigh you down
Ask the Lord to lift you up
For blessed are they who seek higher ground.

Blessed are they that keep his testimonies,
and that seek him with the whole heart.
Psalm 119: 2

FORGIVENESS

Sharp bitter memories that prick the mind
Will sweeten the heart when unforgiveness goes blind.
Let Love's vision search you completely within
To give you clear focus so you can forgive others of sin.

Not through your eyes and not through mine
But through the eyes of our Divine
Lord, help us see each other's worth
As forgiveness in our hearts is birthed.

When fingers from the heart reach out
Through portals of forgiveness without
Saying, "But, maybe, we'll see or if,"
Then forgiveness is Love's genuine gift.

Always remember what the Bible has to say
When others harm or hurt you in any kind of way.
You must forgive others when they sin against you
If you want God's forgiveness, when you sin too.

*14 For if ye forgive men their trespasses, your heavenly Father
will also forgive you: 15 But if ye forgive not men their
trespasses, neither will your Father forgive your trespasses.
St. Matthew 6: 14-15*

*And be ye kind one to another, tenderhearted, forgiving one
another, even as God for Christ's sake hath forgiven you.
Ephesians 4: 32*

FREEDOM'S EMERGENCY (September 11, 2001)

Freedom's emergency on September 11th of '01
Gave birth to our nation's new patriotic son.
Eyes that knew not the wreckage of war
Are filled now with tears those birth pains bore.

Being helpful to others in their own time of need
Our heroes stepped in while their hearts dared to bleed.
The many acts of kindness amidst all the terror
Made us grateful for freedom in this new kind of era.

We'll never forget the day that things went wrong
Or the clouds of black smoke where twin towers belong.
Every victim whose tragedy was media exposed
Is now a hero that each friend of freedom knows.

One nation undivided, forever we'll stand
As we reach out to others, great hand in great hand.
We'll always remember the way our lives used to be
Before terrorists boarded four planes, each to crash a city.

Our country has healed from war wounds before
But our scars lay in graveyards at freedom's door.
Those who were lost in our nation's tragedy
Have helped us to find a new war strategy.

Every citizen of our nation must now stand guard
So our inherited liberties will not get charred.
The sands of our homeland where our footprints appear
Must not have the prints of terrorists coming near.

Our lives are now different as of today
Because we face an ongoing war that won't go away.
The rules are different than those of the past
But remember, the Spirit of America can't be surpassed!

For, brethren, ye have been called unto liberty; only use not
liberty for an occasion to the flesh, but by love serve one another.
Galatians 5: 13

GOD'S GIFTS

Satan's little creepy helpers
Are demonized elves
Looking inside each of us
Searching for our inner selves.

It's not when you expect it
That those devilish scheming imps
Roam around maliciously
Trying to make us spiritual wimps.

Those deceiving little brats
Who come to steal our gifts
That God gave each of us
Are coming to shoplift.

Some people stay afraid
And hand over what God gave them
While others throw their gifts away
As if it's just another item.

There are some that use their gifts
In service to the lives of others
And because they're faithful stewards
God will gift them with another.

The devil will try to steal your gifts
Whether or not they're being used
So find and use those things in you
For unused gifts count as misused.

7 But unto every one of us is given grace according to the measure
of the gift of Christ. 8 Wherefore he saith, When he ascended
up on high, he led captivity captive, and gave gifts unto men.
Ephesians 4: 7-8

GOD'S LIGHT

Why do God's children put their stars
In silent dark caves of night
Instead of hanging them sky-high
As beacons of hope and light?

Why do God's children hide His light
In the crevices of their hearts to keep
Instead of shining the Lord's brilliance
On salvation to guide His lost sheep?

If each of God's children would hang
Their bright and beaming stars up high
His light would chase away the darkness
And hope would fill men's desperate eye.

Take heed therefore that the light which is in thee be not darkness.
St. Luke 11: 35

GOD'S LITTLE SHEEP

God's little sheep come graze on His Word
In fields of green pastures where all lambs are herd.
Living Waters flow freely at salvation's water hole
So thirst no more and come quench your soul.

God's little sheep find forgiveness to their fill
When they freely roam around at Calvary's Hill.
They bask in the "Son" who lights the way of the cross
But some stray into darkness and find themselves lost.

God's little sheep gather daily to pray
For their brothers and sisters that have gone astray.
When one is lost and then is found
There's a great celebration with joyful sound.

God's little sheep follow the sacrificed Lamb
Who is now their Shepherd, called the great I AM.
Just follow the voice of the Living Word
And come into His flock to join this wooly herd.

*Even so it is not the will of your Father which is in
heaven, that one of these little ones should perish.
St. Matthew 18: 14*

GOD'S PLAN

The master plan for each life
Has been skillfully designed
And though something may seem good
It may not be what God had in mind.

God's plan is not necessarily
To be understood for all to see
But because He knows what's best
Let faith guide you to let Him be.

Christ would like for everyone
To have faith in every trial and test
And to learn to trust in Him alone
Where abiding with Him brings rest.

Since everyone's called to minister
To bear His witness of good news
Rise and stand upon your feet
And face your trials while being used.

If your faith produces fruits
How happy the Lord would be
And if those fruits reproduce
Then His bigger plan you'll see!!!

*But rise, and stand upon thy feet: for I have appeared
unto thee for this purpose, to make thee a minister and
a witness both of these things which thou hast seen, and
of those things in the which I will appear unto thee
Acts 26: 16*

GOSPEL GRAPES

Grapevines of the heavenlies
Filled with plump and juicy grapes
Have vines ready to be picked
So God's love can squirt on hate.

Help yourselves to all you want
Of this satisfying snack.
Pick a bunch to give away
For their abundance is not lack.

Gospel grapes are forgiveness red
And sweeter than the rest
For their sugar content is much higher
Because with love each bunch is blessed.

Winepress of the gospel grapes
Gives us Holy Spirit wine
And pressing us to holiness
Are the bottlers of divine.

Drink soberly for His equipping
And in wisdom pick sweet fruit
For the winery of sin's bootleggin'
Uses sour grapes without dispute.

Fruits of your vine, if neglected
Will dry, wilt and have no squirt
So tend the vineyards of your heart
And start "raisin" prayers and be alert.

If grapes are picked from vines of sin
You'll be pressed to judgment by our Divine
Then grapes of wrath will squirt on you
Unless you drink repentance wine.

16 Ye shall know them by their fruits. Do men gather grapes of thorns, or figs of thistles? 17 Even so every good tree bringeth forth good fruit; but a corrupt tree bringeth forth evil fruit. 18 A good tree cannot bring forth evil fruit, neither can a corrupt tree bring forth good fruit. 19 Every tree that bringeth not forth good fruit is hewn down, and cast into the fire.
St. Matthew 7: 16-19

GROANINGS OF THE SOUL

Without meat on the bones of our words
We often have no prayers
But God understands grandeur groanings
And moanings when our words are bare.

The language of the Holy Spirit
Will understand our every cry
And every grunt and groan of the soul
That falls in tearful, longing eye.

God knows each thought and intention
When words have not yet formed
So if you don't know what to pray
The moanings of your soul inform.

*Likewise the Spirit also helpeth our infirmities: for we know
not what we should pray for as we ought: but the Spirit itself
maketh intercession for us with groanings which cannot be uttered.
Romans 8: 26*

GROWING UP ME

Growing up my children
Means growing up me
Because when I see myself in them
I know I'd better act responsibly.

They imitate what I say and do
Just because they're my kids
So it's hard to get mad and blame them
When their actions are not, um…splendid.

Father, in all things help me mimic You
So that my kids mimic You through me.
Then I can honestly and happily say
What proud parents You and I would be!

14 That we henceforth be no more children, tossed to and
fro, and carried about with every wind of doctrine, by the
sleight of men, and cunning craftiness, whereby they lie in
wait to deceive: 15 But speaking the truth in love, may grow
up into him in all things, which is the head, even Christ:
Ephesians 4: 14-15

HALLE-LOOSE-YAHWEH, I'M FREE

Halle-loose-yah, praise the Lord
Halle-loose-yah, I'm free
For the shackles of my sin
Have been loosened from me.

No more chains of the devil
Can be wrapped around my neck.
Halle-lucifer no more
You heard me, that's correct!!!

Now it's Halle-loose-Yahweh my Lord
And Halle-loose-Yahweh my Master.
I sing sweet praises to Your name
For "loose-ing" sin's disaster.

God took the key to loose His Spirit
Which Halle-loose-Yahweh poured on me.
Then He opened up sin's prison doors
That held me captive, now I'm free!!!

Bring my soul out of prison, that I may praise
thy name: the righteous shall compass me
about; for thou shalt deal bountifully with me.
Psalm 142: 7

HANDS OF MINISTRY

I know that I'm a handful
In my own rights, though sometimes wrong
So Lord, do what You must do
To purify me as we go along.

I dedicate my hands to You
To worship, love and serve
And do those things You've called me to
Without complaint or reserve.

The ministry for my hands
Will need strong and healthy arms
Because I'll carry the lost and strayed
To safety from sinful harms.

I pray my hands will be obedient
To do whatever You want them to do.
I'll lift them up to praise Your name
Filled with love just for You.

As my hands reach out to others
I'll be extending Your hand of love
And as I serve them, I'm serving You
Because my hands belong to my Beloved.

Thus will I bless thee while I live:
I will lift up my hands in thy name.
Psalm 63: 4

HIGHER HIGHS

My love for You has grown again
So I hope it brings You smiles.
Each time I reach my lowest spot
I thank You for my trials.

The farther that I drift from You
Higher I'll have to reach
So when I climb up top again
I'm at life's highest peak.

I know for sure You won't leave me
When darkness does arrive
And as I walk through the valleys
I'll think of higher highs.

*The LORD openeth the eyes of the blind: the LORD raiseth
them that are bowed down: the LORD loveth the righteous
Psalms 146: 8*

HIS SANDALS

The King of the Heavens is King of my prayers
Because the thunderous storms that fill our sky
Are but whispers in my Father's ear
Each time the sound of my voice comes near.

My prayers open His throne room doors
Then as His scepter is fully extended He says,
"My child, My child, please come to Me
Make known your innermost plea."

My Lord, my Saviour, my All-In-All
Every request can be summed into one.
All I ask is to wear the sandals of my Lord
So the footprints of my life will duplicate Yours.

The love of my life held me endeared in His arms
Before He put His sandals on me.
Then He happily gazed into my tearful eyes
As He washed my feet to my surprise!

Christ dried my feet with His garment of glory
As He anointed and blessed my life.
Before I left, He said "In all things pray…"
Then He put His sandals on me as I walked away.

I heard His voice behind me say,
"I'll be with you every step that you take.
Come see Me in your prayer life oft
And please don't take My sandals off!"

I turned around to give Him thanks
But He was no longer to be seen.
Then I looked upon my feet in amaze
And saw the outline of His sandals ablaze.

I started praising Jesus, my Lord
Because I know He hears my prayers
And since I knew that I was wearing His shoes
I followed His lead to spread the Good News!

Hold up my goings in thy paths, that my footsteps slip not.
Psalms 17: 5

HOLY GHOST

When eyes of the enemy
Were peering at me
The Holy Ghost said BOO
And boy, did they flee!!!

They were scared out of their wits
And shaking in their shoes.
Thank You, Lord for Your protection
And The Book of Good News.

The enemy ran into hiding
Because there's a Holy Ghost in me
Which means that I have power
To make the devil flee!!!

But ye shall receive power, after that
the Holy Ghost is come upon you;
Acts 1: 8a

HOLY SPIRIT OIL

To get oil out of olives
They must be mashed and squeezed
So Lord, pressurize and extract
My sinful nature, please!

Though the pressure will be great
And the pain will bring me sorrow
My hope is in the extraction
For Holy Spirit oil tomorrow.

Anoint my life with purpose
And anoint each part of me
So that when I'm around others
It's You in me they'll see.

But I am like a green olive tree in the house of
God: I trust in the mercy of God for ever and ever.
Psalm 52: 8

But the anointing which ye have received of him abideth in
you, and ye need not that any man teach you: but as the
same anointing teacheth you of all things, and is truth, and is
no lie, and even as it hath taught you, ye shall abide in him.
I St. John 2: 27

I BELONG TO YOU

My lips belong to You, my Lord
To praise and sing You songs.
I love You so, with all my heart
So let them speak no wrong.

My hands belong to You, my Lord
For helping those in need.
Bless them both so that my touch
Will plant a kingdom seed.

My feet belong to You, my Lord
Guide my path so they won't stray
To the left nor to the right
But that I'll walk straightway.

My eyes belong to You, my Lord
As I look upon creation.
Everything both large and small
Deserves my admiration.

My life belongs to You, my Love
So I dedicate myself to You.
Help me keep Your commandments
And to always be faithful and true.

Let us hear the conclusion of the whole matter: Fear God,
and keep his commandments: for this is the whole duty of man.
Ecclesiastes 12: 13

IN ME

Creator of Creation
Create in me
The gift of
Creativity.

Giver of Gifts
Gift in me
A heart to give
Givingly.

Joy of Morning
Breathe in me
Life worth living
Joyously.

*If ye abide in me, and my words abide in you, ye
shall ask what ye will, and it shall be done unto you.
St. John 15: 7*

IN REMEMBRANCE

Bread of Christ's body
Taken into mine
Stripes of my Saviour
Healer Divine.

Blood of salvation
Upon my lip
Cup of remembrance
I humbly sip.

North to South
Healed to my core
East to West
My sins are no more.

*19 And he took bread, and gave thanks, and brake it, and gave unto
them, saying, This is my body which is given for you: this do in
remembrance of me. 20 Likewise also the cup after supper, saying,
This cup is the new testament in my blood, which is shed for you.*
St. Luke 22: 19-20

INNER PEACE

Lead my heart to the path of joy
So that I may stroll with happiness.
Place my thoughts in the sea of serene
To freely paddle in peace quarantine.

Merge my heart and mind as one
In intimacy to exalt God's Son.
Allow the innermost parts of me
To worship my Lord freely.

Whispered voice of my Divine
Beckons me to inner peace.
He softly asks if I would sit
In stillness, for my benefit.

Away from life's busy-ness
My rest in Him is now assured.
He made a place for my retreat
In the secret place where we meet.

Be still, and know that I am God: I will be exalted
among the heathen, I will be exalted in the earth.
Psalm 46: 10

JUDGMENT BOWL

Rah-rah, hip-hip hooray!
Move the gospel towards our goal.
Be offensive in your moves
For we're headed for the Judgment Bowl.

Spectator saints on the sideline
Watch all the action from the pews.
They proudly shout a-men and pray
But beware, the St. Lukewarm will get spewed.

Those who donned their uniforms
And faced opponents by God's might
Will see the touchdowns that they scored
When the gospel ball transforms to Light.

Our earthly stadium echoes loudly
From the crowds with their jeers or cheers.
While the white team's scoring points for Jesus
The black team's bringing judgment near.

For we must all appear before the judgment seat of Christ;
that every one may receive the things done in his body,
according to that he hath done, whether it be good or bad.
II Corinthians 5: 10

JUST LIKE "THEM"

Aren't you glad you're not like "them"
Those "churchy" sinners considered good folk?
They sit on pews but don't read The Good News
And their part-time religion is just a joke.

Aren't you glad you're not like "them"
Sipping gossip and eating cookies of blame?
Every word that comes out of their mouth
Is prideful and hurtful without shame.

Aren't you glad you're not like "them"
Pretending that they're better than most?
They brag about material things
And fill their conversations with boast.

Aren't you glad you're not like "them"
Those hypocritical church sinners?
They say one thing but do another.
Those losers will never be winners.

Aren't you glad you're not like "them"
Wearing fake smiles on prejudiced lips?
They pretend to be happy but they're not
Because they worship without lordship.

Aren't you glad you're not like "them"
As you go about your merry way?
But just like "them" each day is lived
Judging others till Judgment Day.

*For with what judgment ye judge, ye shall be judged: and
with what measure ye mete, it shall be measured to you again.
St. Matthew 7: 2*

85

JUSTICE SCALES

The justice scales of life
Are tipped out of balance
For the weight of sin from the past
Weighs less than forgiveness vast.

God's heavy hand is on the scales
To prove His love outweighs sin.
When sinful hearts get weighed down
Christ removes each sin pound by pound.

Each time a sinner comes to repentance
Our Saviour tips the justice scales.
Forgiveness makes hearts get lighter
Because His weight of love is mightier.

A just weight and balance are the LORD'S:
all the weights of the bag are his work.
Proverbs 16: 11

KINGDOM HEIRS

Our time on earth is quite a gift
To be unwrapped every day.
We're entrusted daily with its care
To be opened then to share.

If we're faithful in small things of life
Then the big ones will come our way
And in all things if we learn to tithe
His hidden treasures will not hide.

Kingdom heirs we will become
If we live our lives for Christ.
Accept salvation with reward
To have freedom through the Lord.

Fear not, little flock; for it is your Father's
good pleasure to give you the kingdom.
St. Luke 12: 32

LIKE SCENTED INCENSE

Like scented incense are the praises of my heart
Burning with love before the throne of my Beloved.
Inhaling the worship from this vessel of clay
May Your nostrils be filled with its fragrance each day.

Like scented incense is the worship from my lips
Filling the heavenlies with yearning for Thee.
My desires are to sweeten the throne room of Your heart
With songs in my soul that I long to impart.

Like scented incense my thanksgiving to Thee
Will fragrance the aroma of each heartfelt prayer.
My hands lift up filled with praises that flow
For Your sacrifice of love that makes loving You grow.

Like scented incense are my desires for You
Burning with embers of adoration.
While candles of love burn for my Groom
The flame of Your wick lights my bridal room.

Let my prayer be set forth before thee as incense;
and the lifting up of my hands as the evening sacrifice.
Psalms 141: 2

LIP SERVICE

My lips have served You more than I
And been faithful every day.
They always speak loud and clear
But my actions fade away.

If I could serve You like my lips
Then I know that You'd be pleased.
But my heart's not dedicated
And my commitment's just a tease.

Convict my heart to take action
So that my life will leave no doubt
That the truth is not just in my words
But a condition called devout.

The darling duo of words and deeds
Should join together, it's a fact.
So instead of service just from my lips
Lord, let my faith smack me to act!

This people draweth nigh unto me with their mouth, and
honoureth me with their lips; but their heart is far from me.
St. Matthew 15: 8

LIVING FOR TODAY

Living on the hope
That tomorrow we'll see
May find disappointment
For some of them won't be.

There is no promise for tomorrow
So today we must act
And if the hope of tomorrow comes
Teach the two to interact.

When today is passed up for tomorrow
Then it daily ceases to see
That for our next day to be stronger
Our today must learn to be.

Living for today
Is building future dreams
Because the actions of our day-to-day
Lay foundations for support beams.

14 Whereas ye know not what shall be on the morrow. For what is your life? It is even a vapour, that appeareth for a little time, and then vanisheth away. 15 For that ye ought to say, If the Lord will, we shall live, and do this, or that.
James 4: 14-15

LONELY BUT NOT ALONE

Multitudes in loneliness
Seek companionship
But in a world that's so busy
It's hard to find true friendship.

Acquaintances come and go
For very few have time to stay
So it's hard to get to know each other
Past the greetings of the day.

An epidemic of lonely masses
Helps fill empty seats on church pews
Because everyone is searching
For the friendly faces of a few.

Loneliness can bore deep holes
Which eventually taps into
The depths of Holy Spirit waters
That fills wells with joy renewed.

You may be lonely but not alone
So put your searching eyes upon the Lord
And if you spend more time with Him
You'll be best friends as His reward!

*Behold, the hour cometh, yea, is now come, that ye shall
be scattered, every man to his own, and shall leave me alone:
and yet I am not alone, because the Father is with me.
St. John 16: 32*

LOVE MATURE

Right hand of mercy
Left hand of grace
Nailed for salvation
Sin's final resting place.

Forgive them Father
So they may be saved
Voice of Redemption
Raised from the grave.

Life without sin
Death for ours
Lord of Love
Saving powers.

Calvary's carpenter
Royal and pure
Gold filled heart pearls
Love mature.

*34 A new commandment I give unto you, That ye
love one another; as I have loved you, that ye also
love one another. 35 By this shall all men know that
ye are my disciples, if ye have love one to another.
St. John 13: 34-35*

"ME" ATTITUDE

I hunger for Your presence
Yet I only nibble on Your food.
You try to feed "me" with The Word
But my appetite feeds on "me" attitude.

I'm always worried about "me"
And not enough about You.
My thoughts seem to drift away
Each time I pray, though it's few.

"Me" thinks "me" knows what to do
To get "me" out of the way.
I must lay "me" at the cross
And surrender "me-self" each day.

*5 For they that are after the flesh do mind the things
of the flesh; but they that are after the Spirit the
things of the Spirit. 6 For to be carnally minded is
death; but to be spiritually minded is life and peace.
Romans 8: 5-6*

MIRACLES

Moving mountains and walking on the seas
Miracles do happen, God send one please!
Two fish served with five loaves of bread
Fed five thousand bellies in the Bible it is said.

Daniel and the lion's den in days bygone
Noah and the ark with a new morning dawn
The rainbow covenant that still decorates our air
Were miracles like the strength in Samson's uncut hair.

The Jews many miracles before the Promised Land
Like angel bread manna that fed each desert hungry hand
And the Red Sea that parted when Moses raised His staff
Should all be considered a miracle and a half.

The snare of Joshua that made the walls of Jericho fall
And the prison chains that broke off of Silas and Paul
Imagine Jonah living 3 days in the belly of a whale
Should all prove to us that God's miracles can't fail.

Queen Ester's deliverance of the Jews
Ruth, Naomi and Boaz finding love renewed
The defeat of Goliath by David's small stone
Oh, how the hand of God through the ages has shown!!!

A burning bush and the Promised Land
Blind eyes opened and the leper's healed hand
Calming stormy seas without a fuss
Raising the dead??? Ask Lazarus.

Fishing for men in Gospel Lake
And tongues of fire for Pentecost's sake
Joseph's colorful coat and his dreams
Were all miraculous as wild as it seems.

The biggest miracle was the defeat of death
And the love of Christ with endless breath.
As far as the East is to the West
The miracle of forgiveness is the best!!!

*In whom we have redemption through his blood, the
forgiveness of sins, according to the riches of his grace
Ephesians 1: 7*

MIRROR MIRROR

Mirror…mirror… wake up "Sleepy" head
It's time to serve me so get out of bed.
Tell me I'm the fairest in everyone's eyes
Even if it means you must tell me lies.

Mirror…mirror…you're acting so "Dopey"
You're not reflecting anything for me.
I'm looking at darkness and something's wrong
You can't scare me like that, I'm much too strong.

Mirror...mirror...what's going on with you?
Why aren't you focusing all the way through?
There's a bright light that you can't make go dim?
Why don't you "dwarf" the reflection of Him?

Mirror...mirror...you're so "Grumpy" today
It doesn't matter what you have to say!!!
Leave me alone and hide His face from me.
He said I'm poisoned by sin, who is He?

Mirror...mirror...you're too "Bashful" to say
That the Man in the mirror still wants to stay?
Why does He want His reflection in me?
To make me "Snow White" so I can be free?

Mirror…mirror…I feel "Sneezy" and sick
You think the thorn of sin gave me a prick?
Is all of that darkness really my sin?
Forgive me Reflection, please enter in.

Mirror...mirror... you "Doc"-tored me inside
And exposed the evil I tried to hide.
When Jesus stood before me face to face
I denied the One I should have embraced.

"Prince Charming's" reflection now shines in me
Mirrored in love through grace and mercy.
He made me "Snow White" with His kingdom inside.
It's a marriage from Heaven for this bride.

Mirror...mirror... I'm so "Happy" I glow
I'm off to serve Jesus, hi-ho, hi-ho.
He's the apple of my eye and my best friend
So we'll live happily ever-after, without The End.

But we all, with open face beholding as in a glass the
glory of the Lord, are changed into the same image
from glory to glory even as by the Spirit of the Lord.
II Corinthians 3: 18

MY CHILDREN'S GARMENTS
(Dedicated to My Children and Grandchildren)

You have dressed my children in garments of love
So that every time I hold them I'll know of
Your love so grand in these little blessings
And your exquisite taste in fashion dressings.

You have dressed my children in garments of joy
Stitched with happiness that "seams" easy to enjoy.
The hearts of my children spill laughter everywhere
Staining garments of the heart that grown-ups wear.

You have dressed my children in garments of peace
And each time I touch them it's softly released.
Anxieties that chase me day after day
Get chased away by my children when we play.

*That their hearts might be comforted, being knit
together in love, and unto all riches of the full
assurance of understanding, to the acknowledgement
of the mystery of God, and of the Father, and of Christ;
Colossians 2: 2*

MY PRAYER

Guard my thoughts not thought of yet
Before they are conceived.
Let each one come forth from You
So You will not be grieved.

Let each action I display
Tempt others for Your heart.
Bring them back to righteousness
As whole and not just part.

Teach my tongue to be at rest
Quietly in her bed
Listening to the wisdom
Of Your still voice in my head.

And the peace of God, which passeth all understanding,
shall keep your hearts and minds through Christ Jesus.
Philippians 4: 7

MY SINS ARE WASHED AWAY

My nakedness of soul
Exposing all my sins
Was on the cross when Jesus died
But could not be seen by men.

My nakedness of heart
Filled with vile desire
Was cleansed by Christ on the cross
Then clothed with love's attire.

My nakedness of mind
That exposed each thought of sin
Transformed and renewed me
When I let forgiveness in.

My nakedness is clothed
In righteousness and royal array
Because Jesus gave His life for mine
And washed my sins away.

Blessed is he whose transgression
is forgiven, whose sin is covered.
Psalms 32: 1

NEVER SAY NEVER

All the mountains waiting to be climbed
And all the bells waiting to be chimed
Patiently wait but they don't have forever
So enjoy them when you can but never say never.

There are candles waiting to burn their wick
And beautiful flowers waiting to be picked.
Yesterday's minutes we cannot borrow
And we can't multiply time for tomorrow.

Live life to the fullest with goodly fill
And when running on empty, learn to be still.
Nothing in life is impossible through Christ
So when the going gets tough, just ask His advice.

Never say never to opening your eyes
To see the beauty of simple things. Surprise!!!
No matter where you are there are new things unseen
Because each day will have something fresh to glean.

Most importantly, just never say never
To salvation from Christ and His love endeavor.
If you say never to Christ, you'll wish you'd never died
When you cross over to the "other" side.

The earth is the LORD'S, and the fullness
thereof; the world, and they that dwell therein.
Psalm 24: 1

PEARLY GATES
(Dedicated to The Lord)

Gems and jewels are formed in the earth
But pearls are formed inside vessels of life.
They start when intruding particles
Enter within to stir up pain and strife.

Each pearl is formed when an irritant
Gets inside of a living tissue.
It's created by layers of a protective coating
To encase the intruder until it's not an issue.

The end result after much irritation
Is a beautiful pearl exquisitely designed
To teach us that trials that come our way
Will develop within us pearls divine.

The mystery of Heaven's Pearly Gates
Has been waiting in secret to be told
But now is the time that Christ wants us to know
To help each generation become holy and bold.

Since Christ's sufferings on earth have passed
He's eternally celebrated and enthroned.
Twelve huge pearls came forth from His heart
That filled the throne room for His atoned.

He took each pearl and made a beautiful gate
So that as each person passes through,
The remembrance of His sacrificial love
Will forever be in everyone's view.

The trials of our dear Saviour Christ
Were more colossal than our own
Which is why each pearl was so tremendous
And worthy to be doorways to His home.

Thanks to our Lord for His mighty tribulations
That formed Pearly Gates for all twelve tribes
And that the most valuable treasure for anyone
Is that The Book of Life would have your name inscribed.

The Gates of Heaven majestically stand
As a reminder of the sufferings Christ endured
And for those committed to be His followers
Sufferings on earth are also assured.

When we pass through the iridescent Pearly Gates
A marvelous surprise is waiting to be
For we'll find that all of our earthly irritations
Became pearls in our hearts to give back to Thee!

So when your heart feels hurt, pain or trouble
Don't worry about your tribulation trials
Because your heart's busy making lustrous pearls
That will someday bring forth throne room smiles.

Remember each lesson of life's irritants within
Are wrapped with layers upon layers of God working in you.
This makes the protective coating on your pearls unique
Because how you live, determines their value!

Wherefore let them that suffer according to the
will of God commit the keeping of their souls
to him in well doing, as unto a faithful Creator.
I St. Peter 4: 19

And the twelve gates were twelve pearls: every
several gate was of one pearl: and the street of
the city was pure gold, as it were transparent glass.
Revelation 21: 21

PLUMP WORDS OF LIFE

The Bible's filled with words of life
Each plump with joy and peace
Eat a few and watch your gain
As pounds of joyfulness increase.

The weight of inner peacefulness
Though great will make you lighter
Because forgiveness gobbles up our sin
Oh, great is our Delighter!

A belly full of Jesus joy
Will make you plump indeed
And every time you share His Word
Plump is your reward for deeds.

Thy words were found, and I did eat them; and thy
word was unto me the joy and rejoicing of mine heart:
for I am called by thy name, O LORD God of hosts.
Jeremiah 15: 16

POOR ME

In my paradise world it was hard to see
All of God's blessings that had been poured upon me
Until I saw a poor stranger passing by with much lack
Giving his change to help clothe a homeless man's back.

I stood behind my greed as I watched this baffling scene
And was amazed at the generosity my eyes had just seen.
How could someone so poor be kind and willing to share
And in their own misery have compassion for others and care?

HOW and WHY are the unknowns at this point
That have totally dislocated my spiritual joints.
It made no sense until I saw them both pray
And it was then that I knew I was the poor one that day.

When I got home I was still shocked and dazed
Because all I could think of was that poor man's amaze.
It struck me like an arrow that hit the bullseye of my heart
Piercing me to the core whose pain would not depart.

The poor man in me couldn't stop wailing in grief
Until I was finally able to ask the Lord for relief.
I repented with all of my hearts inner man
And asked my Saviour to teach me to help others when I can.

I was flooded with forgiveness and felt different inside
Because I knew that it was my soul that was being purified.
I felt the Lord's love and give thanks He now abides
Where Poor Me used to live but no longer resides.

I'm so grateful the Lord showed me the error of my ways
With His convicting Spirit that follows me all my days.
Poor Me died to self so now I'm no longer poor
Instead I'm filled with riches to share because that's what they're for.

17: But whoso hath this world's good, and seeth his brother
have need, and shutteth up his bowels of compassion
from him, how dwelleth the love of God in him?
I St. John 3: 17

PRAYER COOKIES AND FISH SANDWICHES

I went to the kitchen of my prayers last night
And baked some prayer cookies that were out of sight.
I could not see them but I knew they tasted great
Because sprinkles of forgiveness were left on my plate.

The dough of confession was prepared first
Then adding repentance gave them a flavor burst.
Praise and thanksgiving helped the cookies to rise
As I watched my Lord eat them through my mind's eyes.

Delicious! Delicious! My heart heard Him say
So I've been baking prayer cookies ever since that day.
The Lord said He loves eating homemade treats
But I won't need forgiveness cookies once we meet.

In Heaven I'll bake bread but five loaves is all I'll "knead"
And from its clear riverbed I'll catch two fish then proceed
To prepare fish sandwich platters that have no last bite
And we'll feast on them all day because there is no night.

This miracle meal of Heaven will be garnished with praise
And everyone who eats it will be filled with His amaze
Because the fish taste great when cooked in Holy Spirit oil
But if you prefer sushi, rest assured it will not spoil.

19 When I brake the five loaves among five thousand, how many baskets full of fragments took ye up? They say unto him, Twelve. 20 And when the seven among four thousand, how many baskets full of fragments took ye up? And they said, Seven.
St. Mark 8: 19-20

REFUGE IN THE LORD

Lay not a barren, wounded heart
In open fields of conversation.
If so, its carcass will be found
Picked apart on gossip ground.

Pursue and trust God's sheltered refuge
And restoration He will bring.
He'll renew you through His Living Word
That will soothe and heal the injured.

Seek not comfort when distressed
From casual friends who may turn foe.
Instead reveal your secrets to Him
Because He alone can help you, not them.

I will say of the LORD, He is my refuge
and my fortress: my God; in him will I trust.
Psalm 91: 2

REVIVAL FIRE

Flaming pulpit of revival
Light your fire in each of us.
Burn the pews of indifference
With worship that is fabulous.

Praise our Saviour with renewal
Lord, light Your fire on every tongue.
In Your sanctuary, take thy throne
And enjoy each praise as it's sung.

Our hearts bow before His Majesty
As our voices raise like thunder.
Inhale the worship of revival
For You are worthy, God of Wonder!!!

13 Thy way, O God, is in the sanctuary: who is so great
a God as our God? 14 Thou art the God that doest
wonders: thou hast declared thy strength among the people.
Psalm 77: 13-14

SALT YOUR WORDS

Before you chew on conversation
Select and salt what you want to say
Then place each word upon your tongue
And serve with grace in a righteous way.

Speak in kindness to the lost
And choose wisely from tongue's platter.
Select not just juicy words
That make conversation fatter.

But rather choose plump words of life
That digest easily and fill the heart
Then use the salt that's in God's Word
To season every spoken part.

Preserve your words in truthfulness
And serve each one as if they're dear
So that the flavor of your Godly speech
Will taste better in the listener's ear.

Let your speech be alway with grace, seasoned with salt,
that ye may know how ye ought to answer every man.
Colossians 4: 6

SHIRT TALES
IN MEMORY OF MY DAD, THOMAS RICHARD BEECH, JR.
(August 3, 1921 to August 12, 2005)

The tale of the shirt that I'm going to tell
Really did happen for I remember it well.
After dining on fine food with mom and dad
A young man approached us looking rather sad.

As seen through my eyes he was lonely and poor.
He was asking for money and not a thing more.
When dad told him he'd help, the man's eyes opened wide
But first dad walked us to the car and put us inside.

They entered the restaurant and stayed awhile.
When dad came out I knew he'd gone the extra mile.
My eyes were bewildered when I looked and saw
No shirt on my father as he got in the car.

He said not a word as he took us on home
So I asked him what happened because his heart shone.
Dad let the man order a hot meal from the menu
Then slipped him some cash for his empty pockets too.

T'was a beautiful day with crisp chilly air
But colder to the man whose threads were showing wear.
Dad left him inside so he could warm his limbs
And took both of his shirts off and put them on him.

I'll never forget what he told us that day
That it just wasn't right for things to be that way.
"My closet's full of clothes that I'll never wear
And he needs them more than me so I want to share."

Silence steered us home as our thoughts all drifted
So I'm sure it's safe to say we were each uplifted.
All the way home I just stared at his bare back.
Somehow with no shirt-tails he put my life on track.

The biggest act of kindness I've ever seen
Made me proud that it was my father on the scene.
We don't know whatever happened to that man
But it sure taught me to help whenever I can.

When you read this shirt-tale please whisper a prayer
For the many people who have had to walk there.
Before you finish please pray for all of those
Who reached out to help them and those who gave their clothes.

*And the King shall answer and say unto them, Verily I
say unto you, Inasmuch as ye have done it unto one of
the least of these my brethren, ye have done it unto me.*
St. Matthew 25: 40

SINNING LIPS

When lips are lent to gossip
But they haven't been returned
Words become without conscious
For there's no guidance or discern.

The Lord of truth is not pleased
When He hears chatty gossip or flattery.
Untamed lips of selfish pleasure
Think freedom of speech is free.

There is a price that must be paid
When a tongue has gossip, rant or rave
Or speaks with flattery, anger or lies
Because it receives from what it gave.

Tongue sins are mighty weapons
Used to war against God's light
Because they leave a trail of destruction
As dark words flow from sin's delight.

Seek the Lord for forgiveness
And pray down in the inner core
Lord, please find those sinning lips
Then let them behave and sin no more.

He that goeth about as a talebearer revealeth secrets:
therefore meddle not with him that flattereth with his lips.
Proverbs 20: 19

SOUL SOUP

A piece of joy found in my soup
Was warming to this hungry soul.
As I ate I was pleased to find
Bits of happiness in my bowl.

So I kept stirring with my spoon
To see if more were left behind
And then I found lots of goodness,
Varieties of every kind.

I sipped the broth for nourishment
And tasted His amazing grace.
A soup that was beyond compare
Is finished now without a trace.

So then I read the recipe
(I knew it did not come from home)
And to my amaze this soup was made
From the kitchen where angels roam.

Served at prayer time to meet our needs
It's all imported to our soul
But what I really found is they
Are good in soup but better whole.

Man did eat angels' food: he sent them meat to the full.
Psalms 78: 25

SPARKLING "WHINE"

"Whine" has no sparkle
No bubbly flavor or taste
And though it's not good for you
It gets gulped in impatient haste.

Its partakers act like madmen
Who can't wait to get tongue-drunk
On griping, complaining and "whining"
And anything to dispute or debunk.

Repentance pours the old "whine" out
Into Christ's forgiveness sink
And then He'll fill new "whine-skins"
With good attitudes needed to think.

*13 For it is God which worketh in you both to will and to do
of his good pleasure. 14 Do all things without murmurings
and disputings: 15 That ye may be blameless and harmless,
the sons of God, without rebuke, in the midst of a crooked and
perverse nation, among whom ye shine as lights in the world;
Philippians 2: 13-15*

THAT OLE' SHOVEL

That ole' shovel that dug sin's hole
Knew no boundaries in my life's soil.
Each time I thought I hit the bottom
My shovel dug deeper into turmoil.

My woeful sins have filled my hole
So I have no peace or place to hide.
Each day I leave more muddy tracks
On the trail to find hope inside.

Now my sins are all exposed
Because their hiding hole is overfilled.
Why won't my shovel dig some more
So my shameful sins won't have to spill?

The hole within me though it's full
Has left me feeling miserably empty.
I truly think my shovel's rigged
Because I'm buried alive in captivity.

I can't dig my way back up
Because I'd suffocate in sin
So I began to pray to Christ
To let fresh air and forgiveness in.

My sins have broken up good soil
That's deep within my core
But repentance fertilized the ground
And made it richer than before.

I cast away that wretched tool
(That ole' shovel that dug sin's hole)
Because it tried to bury me alive
But God let it dig just to find my soul.

It is good for me that I have been
afflicted; that I might learn thy statutes.
Psalm 119: 71

THE BEST MEAL

A beggar asked me for a meal
And said, "Sir, don't turn away
For if you feed me one good meal
You'll be blessed today."

I gave the beggar just one meal
But I received a spiritual feast
Because my faith got fattened up with joy
For Christ says to serve the least.

I can chew on joy all day long
For it never loses any flavor
And if you allow me to serve you too
You'll be doing me a great favor.

The best meal I ever had
Was the one I gave away
For it filled my heart with the taste of love
To see a beggar through God's eyes today.

Forgive me Lord for my lack of service
And please bless that hungry one.
Help me always to remember
That by serving others, I serve God's Son.

For I was an hungred, and ye gave me meat: I was thirsty,
and ye gave me drink: I was a stranger, and ye took me in
St. Matthew 25: 35

THE BRIDGE
IN MEMORY OF MY MOM, LOUISE REYNOLDS BEECH
(June 26, 1924 to August 4, 2001)

There's a welcome home celebration just for you.
The Gates of Heaven opened and His promise now comes true.
Go and let your soul be free to enter His domain
While redeemed hearts rejoice and the angels entertain.

Step into God's glory with His shining light on you
As you bask in Heaven's beauty while all things becomes anew.
No more pain...no more sickness...open up your weary eyes
Because you can see forever now into the crystal clear skies.

Love and peace surround you while your healing abounds
As you walk hand-in-hand with Jesus exploring Heaven's grounds.
Enjoy all eternity and do some traveling afar.
See the universe and galaxies, then ride a shooting star.

My love goes with you and is promised forever
So I bid farewell till again we're together.
Someday we'll be joined and meet upon the bridge
Built with a cross and nails upon Heaven's ridge.

Precious in the sight of the Lord is the death of his saints.
Psalms 116: 15

THE CITY'S SHEPHERD

Why is a shepherd standing by me?
This is the 21st century.
There are no sheep in my neighborhood
So I'd herd him out if only I could.

Why is this shepherd smiling at me?
Who in the world could this herder be?
His toes must feel weird in cement fields
So I'm sure he wonders what crops they yield.

Since he wears a robe and carries a staff
Maybe he should stay for a good laugh.
But because he's a misfit and fashion disgrace
He doesn't belong in our comfortable space.

I don't know why I looked in his eyes
But when I did HE was recognized.
It was then my soul knew that He was here
God's gift of salvation standing near.

He embraced me with His loving eyes
While I gazed the scars of my Crucified.
Then quickly He changed as I stood in awe
As He filled me with joy in what I saw.

Every longing I had ever known
Was shining within Him as He shone.
His robe was now glowing in the purest of white
And He was wrapped in rainbows of dancing light.

Now that I know Him I'm not ashamed.
My Shepherd lives I'll proudly proclaim!
So when I see my family, neighbors and friends
I see the flock that He came to tend.

He gathers His sheep to guide them home
Away from sin cities where they roam.
Into pastures of God's heart they're steered
To graze on His Spirit till their body is sheared.

Psalms 23

THIS HOMELESS MAN

There's something about this poor homeless man
That pricks my heart like no other can.
His hands do not beg and he wears a kind smile
Where is his mother? For he's someone's child.

He walks with authority as if a King
But yet he's homeless and doesn't own a thing!
His sandals are worn out and his clothes have holes
But he claims he has new clothes for all of our souls.

He must be crazy but why are the crowds
Listening to him preach, this can't be allowed!
Surely the city council and mayor will meet
To sign an ordinance to protect our streets.

Though he looks harmless, you just never know
What weird behaviors he may start to show.
But when my eyes met his I knew I had to stay
Now I too feel compelled and can't walk away.

The crowds are growing and chanting for more
While waiting for this homeless man at the shelter's door.
People haven't come here in protest or disgust
But to hear this strange man who has gained their trust.

He softly starts speaking and then without delay
The crowds hush from streets even several blocks away.
Every word he speaks is like a bell's toll
That rings within the heart then echoes to the soul.

There's a great awakening being birthed in every heart
For the free gift of salvation and life's fresh new start.
Peaceful crowds began to weep while giving thanks
To this homeless man who speaks so openly and frank.

Rumbles of a mighty shaking started taking place
While he was preaching about forgiveness and grace.
The call to repentance is breaking walls of sin down
Like a revival quake in the heart of this town.

Suddenly this homeless man was covered in a cloud
And as it quickly lifted, beauty mesmerized the crowd
Because he had disappeared into the eyes of nowhere
Leaving trails of sparkling gold dust with healing in the air.

It was at that moment when all our lights came on
That we realized This Homeless Man was really God's Son.
Then the Holy Spirit came and put fire into our eyes
So we could see a glimpse of our Saviour in the skies.

We started understanding that He went back to His home
To rule His kingdom in the skies from His kingly throne.
He told us of His Father and Heaven's Pearly Gates
And that where He lives there's no more sickness, pain or hate.

Everyone was talking of all the things that we had learned
Then we scattered all about to preach and tell of His return.
Now that we have seen Him, we know that it is true
That Jesus is indeed alive and wants to save YOU!!!

For ye know the grace of our Lord Jesus Christ, that
though he was rich, yet for your sakes he became
poor, that ye through his poverty might be rich.
II Corinthians 8: 9

TODAY'S LEPERS

Who are the lepers of the 21st century?
Are they those we have judged to be unworthy?
Could they be ones afflicted from shameful disease?
Or perhaps locked behind bars without liberties?

Could they be God's lambs that got lost along the way
But no one stopped to help them so they went astray?
Where are society's outcasts and downtrod ones?
Are these the lepers on today's horizon?

Who are the ones that have been cast aside?
Some we call drifters because their will has died.
Unclean broken hearts filled with ridicule and disgrace
Cry shameful muddy tears that streak their blank face.

Where are the lepers that are left to stray?
Are they the forgotten homeless with nowhere to lay?
Some wander our streets and some sit on our corners
Asking for change but get laughed at by scorners.

We don't hear rumbles of hunger from their belly's growl
Because we stay away from lepers since their odors are fowl.
If we wouldn't turn our backs, perhaps a life we would save
Then we could share Jesus and spare their soul from hell's grave.

Where are the lepers that are drowning in sin?
Do our churches allow them to enter in?
Sins of darkness gladly reach out to them all
Embracing them tighter after each fall.

When church people ignore and shun lepers of sin
The heart of evil opens and lets all the lepers in.
Accepting to all with no prejudice to impart
Sin does have a big but deceitful, hard heart.

Sin made them feel loved in a deceiving way
While stealing their souls during foul play.
False hope of lepers poured into vials of addiction
Hides them from truth in hopeless affliction.

Sin's epidemics are tearing families apart
With apathy and coldness from the leper's heart.
But just like in bible times of our ancestors from the past
Jesus is alive to heal lepers and love the outcasts!!!

31 And Jesus answering said unto them,
They that are whole need not a physician;
but they that are sick. 32 I came not to call
the righteous, but sinners to repentance.
St. Luke 5: 31-32

TREASURE CHEST

The Lord dug for treasures beneath my flesh
And to my surprise found a treasure chest!
It was filled with rocks that He polished up
Now I'm shining with jewels that don't corrupt.

Love, joy and peace are protective gems
And I'll wear them all in honor of Him.
So when Christ starts to dig a breakthrough ditch
Remember each painful dig will make you rich.

Don't get discouraged when He's picking on you
Because it just means that He's not through.
Each time His pick is picking to break up a rock
More jewels He'll find so don't make Him stop.

But we have this treasure in earthen vessels, that the
excellency of the power may be of God, and not of us.
II Corinthians 4: 7

WHEN I GO TO HEAVEN

When I go to Heaven
Will there be anyone
Who can thank me for an act of kindness
That on earth I may have done?

Did I make a difference
To anyone in the world?
Did I intercede for others
To help them through The Gates of Pearl?

Has anyone gone to Heaven
Because the gospels I did share?
Or did I pass up opportunity
Because of selfish care?

Lord, let me start anew today
To bring glory to Your name.
I'll spread good news of salvation
And help the sick, poor and lame.

*19 Brethren, if any of you do err from the truth, and
one convert him; 20 Let him know, that he which
converteth the sinner from the error of his way, shall
save a soul from death, and shall hide a multitude of sins.
James 5: 19-20*

"WISH"-MAS LIST

'Tis the season of our folly
Ha-ha, hee-hee, ho-ho.
I'll buy me this and you buy me that
It's off to shop we go.

Here's a gift to me from Santa
(I'll be sure to act surprised)
And when I take the bow off
I'll open wide my eyes.

Here you go, this one's from you
I'll turn my head while you pay.
Wrap it pretty in a bright, big box
To be opened on Christmas Day.

Now, let's see, more gifts for me
I'm gallivanting all over town.
Like a comet from the Heavens
Credit cards are shooting me down.

I better watch out so I don't cry
When the bills start coming in.
I'll open them up after Christmas
And for now ignore this expensive sin.

It will be a Merry Christmas
As my wish-mas list does grow
So I'll apply for another plastic
Ha-ha-hee-hee-ho-ho.

I bought myself a nativity scene
Because…welllllll…it's appropriate.
I guess I'll feel better Christmas Day
If I make myself glance at it.

Christmas morn has now passed through
And all my wrapped gifts are gone
So I'll take a peek at baby Jesus
Before I take a nap…yawn, yawn.

I looked at the nativity set
With baby Jesus in His crib
When suddenly I felt a pain
Pricking me beneath my rib.

Somehow, something or someone
Was tugging at my heart strings
And was asking me a question…
Did good cheer for me I bring???

I went to bed to sleep this off
In hopes that prick would somehow leave
But when I laid upon my pillow
A ton of bricks my head received.

It was strange the way it happened
But somehow my eyes were opened wide
So I could see the real meaning of Christmas
Which I guess I've always tried to hide.

With my seeing eyes now opened
I could clearly see my wrongs
So I repented to my Saviour
And put Christmas where it belongs.

The next day I returned my stuff
That I would never ever use
But I proudly wore my new heart from Jesus
And my brand new pair of destiny shoes.

They were a perfect size and perfect fit
And I'll always wear my destiny pair
Because their color is salvation red
To remind me that I'm a kingdom heir.

My wish-mas list has now changed
And I'll show Christ how much I care
So every day will be like Christmas
And jolly I'll be as I serve and share.

Life is fun when helping others
So it's off to shopping I go.
It's all for them and not for me
Ha-ha-hee-hee-ho-ho.

21 And she shall bring forth a son, and thou shalt call his
name JESUS: for he shall save his people from their sins.
22 Now all this was done, that it might be fulfilled which was
spoken of the Lord by the prophet, saying, 23 Behold, a virgin
shall be with child, and shall bring forth a son, and they shall
call his name Emmanuel, which being interpreted is, God with us.
St. Matthew 1: 21-23

WORRY WORMS

Worry worms know the way
To inch back in our life
But if their food source is cut off
They'll go elsewhere to feed on strife.

Quit worrying and they will leave
Then the garden of your life will grow.
Bear fruit upon the vine of Christ
As you watch each worry worm go.

As blooms of faith start peeking through
Little wiggle worms start to scatter.
They're trying to leave in a hurry
Before a step in faith makes them *SPLATTER*!!!

(For we walk by faith, not by sight:)
II Corinthians 5: 7

YOU'RE FIRED!!!

Self and flesh, you're fired!!!
You're trumped by the Spirit of God
So pack your bags with all you can hold
Because you're being "fired" to bring forth gold.

It's time for you to leave my life
So layer by layer you'll now burn up
Because you can't enter through Heaven's gate
Since God incinerates selfishness and hate.

No matter what you think or say
You have no worth to trust in
But repentance to Christ will let me trade
My rags for riches and they're all pre-paid!!!

And I will bring the third part through the fire, and will
refine them as silver is refined, and will try them as gold is
tried: they shall call on my name, and I will hear them: I will
say, It is my people: and they shall say, The LORD is my God.
Zechariah 13: 9

CPSIA information can be obtained
at www.ICGtesting.com
Printed in the USA
LVOW03s1702180917

549114LV00025B/1737/P